Howlers

and Other New World Monkeys

Concept and Product Development: Editorial Options, Inc.
Series Designer: Karen Donica
Book Author: Mary E. Reid

**For information on other World Book
products, visit us at our Web site at
http://www.worldbook.com**

**For information on sales to schools and libraries
in the United States, call 1-800-975-3250.**

**For information on sales to schools and libraries
in Canada, call 1-800-837-5365.**

World Book, Inc.
233 N. Michigan Avenue
Chicago, IL 60601

Library of Congress Cataloging-in-Publication Data

Reid, Mary E.
    Howlers and other New World monkeys / [book author, Mary E. Reid].
      p. cm.—(World Book's animals of the world)
    Summary: Questions and answers explore the world of New World monkeys, with an
    emphasis on howler monkeys.
    ISBN 0-7166-1209-7 -- ISBN 0-7166-1200-3 (set)
    1. Howler monkeys—Juvenile literature. 2. Cebidae—Juvenile literature. [1. Howler
    monkeys—Miscellanea. 2. Monkeys—Miscellanea. 3. Questions and answers.] I. World Book,
    Inc. II. Title. III. Series.

QL737.P925 R35 2000
599.8'5—dc21   00-021639

Printed in Singapore

1 2 3 4 5 6 7 8 9 05 04 03 02 01 00

ıimals of the World

Howlers
and Other New World Monkeys

What's all the howling about?

Contents

What kind of spider doesn't spin a web?

Do I blow bubbles?

Who-o-o is a night owl?

What Is a Howler?

A howler is a kind of monkey. There are many different species, or kinds, of monkeys. All monkeys belong to one of two groups: New World monkeys or Old World monkeys. Howlers are New World monkeys. Capuchins *(KAP yu chihnz)* and marmosets *(MAHR muh zehts)* are New World monkeys, too.

Howlers are some of the largest New World monkeys. Male howlers are much larger than females. Adult males weigh from 12 to 20 pounds (5.4 to 9 kilograms) and are 2 feet (61 centimeters) long. That's not counting their tails—they're as long as their bodies!

Most howlers have black, brown, or reddish fur. In one species of black howlers, adult males are black and females are golden.

Howlers, like most monkeys, can grasp objects or branches with both their hands and feet. Howlers have thumbs that are almost as nimble as human thumbs. Howlers can use the big toes on their feet like thumbs, too.

Black howler pair

Where in the World Do New World Monkeys Live?

New World monkeys live in parts of North America, Central America, and South America. Howlers live in a wider range than any other New World monkey—from southern Mexico to southeastern Brazil.

Howlers also live in more types of habitats than any other group of New World monkeys. They live in rain forests, thorny forests, swamp forests, and misty forests, high in the mountains.

Mantled howlers prefer to live in old-growth forests that have very old and very big trees. Red howlers live in old-growth forests, too. But these monkeys also live in forests made of young trees. Brown howlers like mountain forests. Red-handed howlers like forests that flood.

World Map

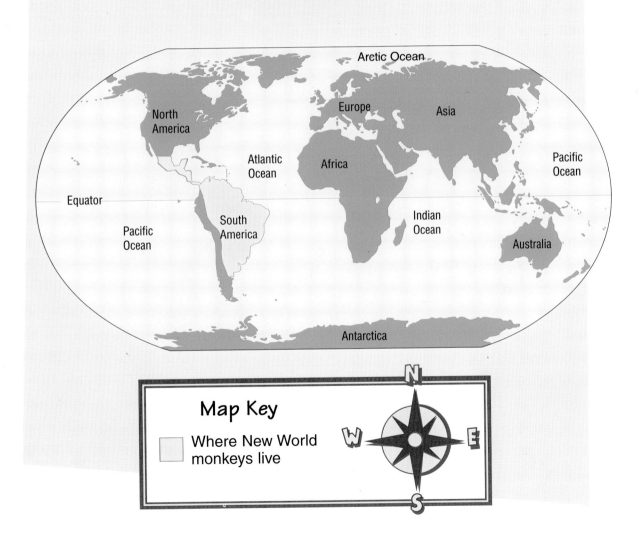

Arctic Ocean

North America

Europe

Asia

Atlantic Ocean

Africa

Pacific Ocean

Equator

Pacific Ocean

South America

Indian Ocean

Australia

Antarctica

Map Key

Where New World monkeys live

N
W E
S

How Are New World and Old World Monkeys Different?

New World monkeys and Old World monkeys differ in many ways. One way is where they live. New World monkeys live from Mexico in North America to Brazil in South America. Old World monkeys live in Africa and Asia.

One way to tell these monkeys apart is by looking at their noses. New World monkeys have flat noses and nostrils that are spaced far apart. Old World monkeys have narrower noses.

All New World monkeys have tails. Some have prehensile *(pree HEHN suhl)*, or grasping, tails. Not all Old World monkeys have tails. Old World monkeys do not have prehensile tails.

All New World monkeys live in trees. Some New World monkeys come to the ground, but not for very long. Many Old World monkeys live on the ground.

Red howler

Where Do Howlers Hang Out?

Howlers hang out very high up in treetops. They spend most of their time in the middle or at the top of the forest canopy. The canopy is a covering formed by the crowns, or tops, of trees. Howlers are definitely not afraid of heights!

Howlers, like some other New World monkeys, have prehensile tails. A howler can use its strong, flexible tail as a fifth hand. The tail is so powerful that a howler can hang by it alone! The underside of the tip has bare skin instead of fur. A howler can use this area to feel things, just as we use the palms of our hands.

Howlers climb and walk around the vines and treetops on all four feet. They move slowly and carefully. Howlers wrap their tails around tree trunks and branches as they go. This helps them keep a safe grip.

Black howler

Who's Who in a Howler Troop?

Howlers live in groups that usually have 15 to 20 members. The group is called a troop. Each troop normally has several adult males, a larger number of adult females, and young ones of different ages.

Members of the troop keep watch over one another. They warn each other when they spot a predator.

A dominant male, which is usually the largest howler, is the troop leader. He gets a lot of attention and affection. He also has first choice of food and mates. Each troop may also have a female that is dominant over other females in the group.

When young male howlers are fully grown, they usually leave the troop. They may join another troop or start their own. This gives them a chance to become leaders. This also helps keep the first troop peaceful. If a howler troop has too many young males, fights may break out.

Howler troop

Why Do Howlers Howl?

Howlers have many reasons for their loud howls. Often, adult males begin their day by howling. They're not just clearing their throats, either. Their howls can be heard as far as 2 miles (3.2 kilometers) away! The monkeys announce their location with morning howls to other howlers. These howls also warn other troops to stay away from their territory.

Howlers also roar when they are disturbed or when two groups of howlers meet. Sometimes this leads to a fight. Their booming calls warn the troop when predators are nearby, too.

Howler monkeys have special structures in their throats that help make their calls so loud. These structures are hollow and egg-shaped, and they act like echo chambers. They are even larger in males, so their voices are louder and deeper.

Howler howling

How Do Howlers Keep Clean?

Howlers keep clean by lending each other a helping hand. Howlers, like some other New World monkeys, groom each other. They clean each other's fur by combing it with their fingers. They carefully pick out bits of leaves, bark, ticks, and insect eggs that they find.

Usually females do most of the grooming. They groom mainly relatives and infants. Grooming each other isn't just good for their looks. Howlers enjoy being groomed. Grooming one another brings howlers closer together, too.

Red, black, and brown howlers spend more time grooming than other howlers.

Howlers grooming

What Do Howlers Eat?

Howlers often eat leaves while hanging from a branch. Leaves make up nearly half of a howler's diet. Other New World monkeys do not eat so many leaves.

Small, young leaves are the favorites of howlers. These leaves are tender and have many nutrients. Howlers also eat flowers and fruit.

Howlers get most of the water they need by eating juicy leaves. But when these monkeys do drink, they can usually find water way up in the canopy. Water often collects in places such as tree holes. Howlers reach their hands into these puddles and then lick their fingers. If howlers are really thirsty, they will go to the forest floor and drink right from a pond or stream.

Red howler

Are Howlers Always Sleepy?

You might think so if you followed one around all day! Howlers are among the least active of all monkeys. They sleep all night and spend about 8 to 10 hours a day resting. That's a lot of naps!

Howlers spend the rest of the time finding food and eating. It's a good thing they like to eat a lot of leaves! Howlers can find leaves just about anywhere.

Black howler

How Do Howler Babies Grow Up?

A howler mother gives birth to one baby at a time. She raises it on her own. The baby grabs onto its mother's fur and begins nursing, or drinking its mother's milk. At first, the baby clings to its mother's belly with its hands and feet. When it is a month old, it begins to use its tail, too.

At 2 months, a howler baby begins to ride on its mother's back. While she rests, the baby may drop from her back and go off exploring on its own. But as soon as its mother gets up, the baby rushes back to her. It still clings to her belly at night.

While it is still very young, the howler gets to know the rest of the group. The other howlers begin noticing the baby, too. Adult howlers in the group are usually very gentle with young ones. Adult males even allow babies to climb all over them!

Young howlers like to play. As they grow older, they like to chase one another. They also like to hang by their tails and play fight with each other.

Black howler mother and baby

Which New World Monkeys Are Named After Monks?

Capuchin monkeys are named after an order of monks that originated in Italy. These monks wear hoods. A capuchin monkey has a dark patch of hair on its head. Some people think this patch looks like the hood that the monks wear!

Capuchins are smaller than howlers. Capuchins are about 17 inches (43 centimeters) long and have 18-inch (46-centimeter) tails. Capuchins weigh much less, too—only about 5 pounds (2.3 kilograms). Most are black or brown, with light-colored hair on their faces.

Capuchins are much more active than howlers. Capuchins move around like acrobats—climbing, running, hopping, and leaping among the trees.

Except for a midday nap, capuchins spend almost all day looking for food. They have a lot of choices, too! They eat almost anything—from fruit, nuts, flowers, and leaves to insects, birds, lizards, squirrels, and oysters.

Capuchin

Just How Smart Are Capuchins?

Many scientists believe that capuchins are the most intelligent New World monkeys. Capuchins are so smart that they are taught to help physically challenged people with daily activities. Capuchins can be trained to help open things or reach items that disabled people cannot.

Unlike most New World monkeys, capuchins use tools in the wild. They use twigs to capture insects that live in small holes in trees. They use rocks to smash nuts open. Capuchins also hunt and eat other foods that are hard to find. For example, capuchins rip bark off trees to find sleeping geckos, hiding spiders, and giant cockroaches. They pick over dead leaves to find insects, too.

Tufted capuchin

How Do Capuchins Get Along?

Capuchins live in large groups of up to 30 monkeys. A dominant male is in charge of the group. Usually he is the largest and oldest male. He doesn't really keep order, though. He usually doesn't need to, either. Capuchins get along very well with one another.

But a dominant male capuchin does have some very important responsibilities. The other monkeys in the group watch their leader's activities closely. They travel when he travels. They rest when he rests. They eat when he eats.

Like many howler troops, capuchins also have a dominant female. Lower-ranking females spend a lot of time grooming her. This keeps them in close, friendly contact.

Capuchins

Which New World Monkey Stays Up at Night?

Night monkeys are the world's only monkeys that are nocturnal, or active at night. They are also called owl monkeys—and with good reason. Like owls, they have large eyes that are well adapted for seeing at night. Like owls, they make hooting noises.

Night monkeys eat mainly ripe fruit. They like flowers, leaves, and insects, too. Feeding at night may allow night monkeys to avoid competing with other monkeys for food. Night monkeys can also hunt and eat insects that come out only at night.

Night monkeys live in all kinds of forests, from Panama to Paraguay. They especially like forests with vines. Often they will sleep all day in a tangle of vines.

Night monkey

What Is Family Life Like for Night Monkeys?

Unlike many other New World monkeys, night monkeys are monogamous *(muh NOHG uh muhs)*. That means that adults have one mate at a time. Night monkeys are even believed to keep one mate for life. A female night monkey gives birth to just one baby a year. The father helps to raise the baby— which is unusual among monkeys. The baby spends much of its first several months under its father's care.

Gradually, the baby begins to spend more time with its mother and older brothers and sisters. Soon, it becomes familiar with everyone in the family.

During the day, a family of night monkeys sleeps nestled together. At dusk, they awaken and stretch. Then the parents lead the family from the tree. They climb along vines in single file as they search for food in the dark. If family members separate, they stay in touch by hooting.

Night monkeys

35

How Many Sounds Do Squirrel Monkeys Make?

Squirrel monkeys make as many as 26 different calls. They sure are noisy! Many of the noises sound like clucks or peeps to us. But squirrel monkeys can tell these calls apart. These monkeys make certain sounds for certain purposes.

Most of the time, females make all the noises. Sometimes it sounds almost as if they are talking. They use clucks to tell others where they are as they travel through the forest. They can probably recognize each other's voices, too.

Females use peeps to tell their infants when to start and stop nursing. They also make comforting noises while they are nursing. Squirrel monkeys make other sounds when they feel aggressive and when they sense danger.

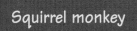
Squirrel monkey

How Big Are Squirrel Monkey Troops?

Squirrel monkeys form larger groups than do other New World monkeys. Squirrel monkeys usually live in groups of 10 to 50 monkeys. But deep in the Amazon rain forests, people have reported seeing groups of 500 squirrel monkeys!

Squirrel monkeys spend their days doing a little bit of everything. They eat insects and ripe fruit. They travel to find new locations where there is plenty of food available. They rest and sleep, too. Usually they do all this in small, all-male or all-female groups. One thing they don't do very often is groom one another. That may be because they are just too busy!

Squirrel monkey troop

How Shaggy Are Sakis?

Sakis *(SAK eez)* are some of the shaggiest monkeys around. Their bodies are about 18 inches (46 centimeters) long and are covered with thick fur. Sakis have tails that are slightly longer but just as shaggy as their bodies. Fur and all, sakis weigh about 4 pounds (1.8 kilograms).

But all that fur doesn't seem to slow sakis down. They walk, climb, and run on four legs through the canopy. They can also leap as far as 32 feet (9.75 meters)! Sakis are sometimes called "flying monkeys" because of their amazing leaping ability.

White-faced saki

What Makes Red Uakaris Unique?

The bright red faces and nearly bald heads of red uakaris *(wah KAHR eez)* are unique among monkeys. Some scientists believe they can tell how healthy a red uakari is by looking at its face. The redder its face, the healthier it is.

Their faces are not the only things that make red uakaris and other uakaris unique. Their tails are unusual, too. They have short, bushy tails—unlike other New World monkeys. When uakaris are excited, they wag their stubby tails heartily.

Uakaris are about 19 inches (48 centimeters) long with tails nearly 7 inches (18 centimeters) long. They weigh about 9 pounds (4.1 kilograms). These monkeys live in the treetops of swamp forests. During the dry season, they come to the ground to search for seeds and young plant shoots to eat.

Red uakari

Does a Spider Monkey Have Eight Legs?

No, it has just two! But when this monkey hangs by its four limbs and tail, it really does look like a huge spider. Spider monkeys have bodies about 18 inches (46 centimeters) long. Their tails are even longer—over 2 feet (61 centimeters). These monkeys weigh around 15 pounds (6.8 kilograms).

Spider monkeys are excellent climbers. They travel around the treetops, swinging swiftly from branch to branch. They use their extremely long, flexible tails to help them, too. They are among the fastest and most agile New World monkeys.

Ripe fruit is the favorite food of spider monkeys. They also eat bark, leaves, and buds. Spider monkeys spend about half their day feeding and traveling. They spend the other half resting.

44

Spider monkey

Are Woolly Monkeys Really Woolly?

Woolly monkeys are very woolly! They get their name from their thick, soft fur. Woolly monkeys live high up in mountain habitats. Their heavy coats help keep them warm in cold weather.

Woolly monkeys are quite large, too. Their bodies are about 15 to 23 inches (38 to 58 centimeters) long. Their tails are slightly longer than that. Woollies weigh from 10 to 20 pounds (4.5 to 9 kilograms). An adult woolly monkey may eat 1/3 of its weight in food each day. (A 60-pound child would need to eat 80 hamburgers to have 1/3 of his or her weight in a day.) That's a lot of fruits and seeds!

Woolly monkeys are very peaceful. Although different troops sometimes share parts of their territories, they rarely fight over food. Instead, adult woolly monkeys spend a lot of time grooming one another. While the adults are busy grooming, young woolly monkeys are busy playing. Sometimes older monkeys join in the fun, too.

Woolly monkey

How Do Titis Stick Together?

Titis *(tih TEEZ)* sometimes seem to be stuck together with glue! These little monkeys are about 15 inches (38 centimeters) long and weigh 2 1/4 pounds (1 kilogram). They live in small, tight-knit families in tropical rain forests.

Much of the time, titis sit and hug one another. They twine their tails together, too. They also twine their tails when they are grooming and sleeping. Titi families sleep huddled together in a tangle of vines.

Male and female titis mate for life. Each morning, father and mother titis call out a long duet. These calls declare their territory to other titi families. Most of the time, the father carries the baby. The father shares food and plays with the baby, too.

Bolivian titis

How Big Are Muriquis?

Muriquis are the largest New World monkeys. Their bodies are 30 inches (76 centimeters) long, and their tails are just as long. These monkeys weigh around 33 pounds (15 kilograms).

Muriquis are among the most peaceful New World monkeys. Males hardly ever get upset with one another. When these monkeys do have arguments, they prefer not to fight. Instead, they make noises until one of them backs off.

Muriquis rarely groom each other. But they do embrace each other for comfort. When muriquis meet a friend of the same sex, they greet each other with a hug.

Muriqui

How Small Are Pygmy Marmosets?

Pygmy marmosets are the smallest New World monkeys. A pygmy marmoset can fit on an adult human's hand. It is 5 1/2 to 6 1/2 inches (14 to 16 centimeters) long and weighs 5 to 7 ounces (142 to 198 grams).

Unlike most New World monkeys, pygmy marmosets and other marmosets have claws instead of fingernails. They can cling to bark and climb tree trunks—just as squirrels do.

Pygmy marmosets, like all marmosets, usually have twins. Caring for two babies is a big responsibility. Once the babies are a few days old, the mother allows the older brothers and sisters to carry the babies. The father helps, too. He keeps close watch when the young ones begin to explore on their own.

Pygmy marmoset

What Kind of Gum Do Marmosets Chew?

Many marmosets eat tree gum. That is the sticky stuff that oozes out of a tree to seal injuries when its bark has been cut. Marmosets do not chew gum to blow bubbles, though! Tree gum is nutritious. It is always available, too—even when there is a drought and fruit is hard to find.

Marmosets get the gum by holding onto a tree trunk with their claws. They gouge holes in the bark with sharp teeth, which are specially adapted for this purpose. Then they eat the gum that flows from the hole.

Marmosets go back to the same holes day after day. They can do this for a long time without damaging the trees. If the supply gets thin, the marmosets move on to another area.

Marmosets also eat insects and small fruit. Pygmy marmosets eat tree gum more often than other marmosets eat it.

Tassel-eared marmoset

Do Lion Tamarins Roar?

Lion tamarins do not roar, but they do make a lot of other sounds. They whistle, cheep, whine, and even cluck. A golden lion tamarin is a striking-looking monkey. It has long, flowing golden-yellow hair and a mane—much as lions do.

But it sure isn't as big as a lion! Most tamarins are around 12 inches (31 centimeters) long. Their tails are 17 inches (44 centimeters) long. These monkeys weigh about 2 pounds (900 grams).

Lion tamarins live in the lower part of old-growth forests, from about 15 to 30 feet (4.6 to 9 meters) up. Their main food is fruit. They also eat nectar, flowers, insects, and small reptiles. Tamarins look for insects and lizards in leaf litter, in vine tangles, under tree bark, and in plants that grow among tree branches.

Like marmosets, tamarins usually have twins. To help the babies get a balanced diet, parents share food with them.

Golden lion tamarin

Do Emperor Tamarins Rule or Share Their Land?

They share! Emperor tamarins share their land with saddleback tamarins. This sort of cooperation is very rare in nature. But these monkeys have found a way to benefit by living with each other.

To start a mixed troop, one group of tamarins calls out to find another. When the two groups join, there are more members to watch for predators. This larger troop also has an easier time defending its territory from other troops. The members of the mixed group stay in contact by making more loud calls.

Although the larger troop can protect its members and territory better, it also has more mouths to feed. But scientists believe that each kind of tamarin likes to feed at different heights in the canopy. This means that the two types of tamarins don't have to fight over food.

Two other types of tamarins, moustached and red-bellied, are also known to live with saddlebacks.

Emperor tamarin

Are New World Monkeys in Danger?

Many New World monkeys are in danger. Some, such as muriquis and lion tamarins, are near extinction. Many New World monkeys have lost much of their habitat. People have cut down the trees in forests to get lumber and to clear land for farming. When monkeys lose their homes, they have nowhere else to go.

It is not easy for scientists to study some species of New World monkeys. Some live very high up in treetops. Other monkeys live in far off areas that are difficult to get to. Without knowing how some New World monkeys live, it is hard for scientists to learn how to protect them.

Even today, scientists are discovering new species. And they are gradually learning more and more about how other New World monkeys live. As people get to know about New World monkeys, it is hoped that they will be able to protect these animals and their habitats.

Baby golden
lion tamarin

New World Monkey Fun Facts

→ The southern red-necked night monkey is more than twice as active during a full moon.

→ The golden lion tamarin is one of the few monkeys that has been reintroduced to its natural habitat from captivity.

→ The yellow-tailed woolly monkey was believed to be extinct for 50 years. But in 1974, a few of these rare monkeys were found in the mountains of South America.

→ A squirrel monkey has a prehensile tail only when it's an infant.

→ Most New World monkeys have 36 teeth. All Old World monkeys have 32 teeth.

→ Capuchins have been known to hunt frogs that live in bamboo stems. Capuchins may consider frogs a prize catch—they rarely share them with others in their group.

→ Spider monkeys don't have thumbs.

Glossary

adapted Changed to be good for doing something.

adult A fully grown animal.

bark The strong outside covering on the trunk, branches, and roots of trees.

canopy A rooflike covering made by treetops.

claw A sharp, hooked nail on an animal's foot.

cling To hold on tightly.

dominant Ruling and most powerful.

extinction The act of killing off completely.

flexible Able to bend without breaking.

fur Two layers of hair that cover the skin of certain animals. The bottom layer is softer and thicker than the top layer.

gouge To cut out a hole in wood.

groom To take care of appearance.

habitat An animal's home.

howl To give a long, loud yell.

leap To jump gracefully into the air.

mane The long, heavy hair on the back or neck of some animals.

New World monkeys Monkeys that live from Mexico to Brazil.

nimble Moving quickly and lightly.

nocturnal Active at night.

nutrient Food for growing.

Old World monkeys Monkeys that live in parts of Africa and Asia.

predator An animal that eats other animals.

prehensile Good for grasping or holding on to something.

species A group of the same kind of animals.

territory The place that animals keep for themselves only.

troop The name for a group of monkeys and certain other kinds of animals.

vines Plants with long, thin stems that grow along the ground or climb higher.

Index

(**Boldface** indicates a photo, map, or illustration.)

Picture Acknowledgments: Front & Back Cover: © Wolfgang Bayer, Bruce Coleman Inc.; © Christer Fredriksson, Bruce Coleman Collection; © Luis Claudio Marigo, Bruce Coleman Collection; © Norman Owen Tomalin, Bruce Coleman Inc.; © Gunter Ziesler, Bruce Coleman Collection.
© Wolfgang Bayer, Bruce Coleman Inc. 3, 5, 17, 53; © Erwin & Peggy Bauer, Bruce Coleman Inc. 29, 47, 51; © Stephen Dalton, Photo Researchers 5, 33; © Gregory J. Dimijian, Photo Researchers 31; © Kenneth W. Fink, Bruce Coleman Inc. 49; © Christer Fredriksson, Bruce Coleman Collection 59; © Patricio Robles Gil, Bruce Coleman Inc. 23; © François Gohier, Photo Researchers 19; © IFA-Bilderteam/IFA from Bruce Coleman Inc.15; © Zig Leszczynski, Animals Animals 39; © Renee Lynn, Photo Researchers 27; © Luis Claudio Marigo, Bruce Coleman Collection 4, 45; © Tom McHugh, Photo Researchers 25; © Raymond A. Mendez, Animals Animals 21; © Claus Meyer, Minden Pictures 43; © Barry Sweet, AP/Wide World 61; © Norman Owen Tomalin, Bruce Coleman Inc. 11, 37, 57; © Jim Tuten, Animals Animals 35; © Peter Weimann, Animals Animals 41; © Rod Williams, Bruce Coleman Inc. 55; © Gunter Ziesler, Bruce Coleman Collection 7, 13.

Illustrations: WORLD BOOK illustration by Karen Donica 9, 62.